62745

BOOKS BY ROBERT PENN WARREN

John Brown: The Making of a Martyr
Thirty-six Poems
Night Rider
Eleven Poems on the Same Theme
At Heaven's Gate
Selected Poems, 1923–1943
All the King's Men
Blackberry Winter
The Circus in the Attic
World Enough and Time
Brother to Dragons
Band of Angels
Segregation: The Inner Conflict in the South
Promises: Poems 1954–1956
Selected Essays
The Cave
All the King's Men (play)
You, Emperors, and Others: Poems 1957–1960
The Legacy of the Civil War
Wilderness
Flood
Who Speaks for the Negro?
Selected Poems: New and Old, 1923–1966
Incarnations: Poems 1966–1968
Audubon: A Vision
Homage to Theodore Dreiser
Meet Me in the Green Glen
Or Else—Poem/Poems 1968–1974
Democracy and Poetry
Selected Poems: 1923–1975
A Place to Come To
Now and Then: Poems 1976–1978

NOW AND THEN
Poems 1976–1978

NOW AND THEN

Poems 1976–1978

Robert Penn Warren

Random House New York

Some of these poems originally appeared in *The Atlantic Monthly,
The Georgia Review, Ironwood, The New York Review of Books,
The Ohio Review, Quest 77, Saturday Review, The Southern
Review, The Times Literary Supplement, The Yale Review.*

The following poems appeared originally in *The New Yorker*:
"American Portrait: Old Style," "Red-Tail Hawk and Pyre of
Youth," "First Dawn Light," "Little Black Heart of the Telephone,"
"Last Laugh," "Inevitable Frontier," and "Heart of the Backlog."

Library of Congress Cataloging in Publication Data

Warren, Robert Penn, 1905–
    Now and then. Poems 1976–1978.

    I. Title.
PS3545.A748N6   811'.5'2   78–57102
ISBN 0–394–50164–0
      0–394–73515–3 pbk
      0–394–50220–5 ltd.

Manufactured in the United States of America

9 8 7 6 5 4 3 2

FIRST EDITION

To Andrew Vincent Corry

... let the inhabitants of the rock sing ...

ISAIAH 42:11

Contents

I
NOSTALGIC

* This symbol is used to indicate a space between sections of a poem wherever such spaces are lost in pagination.

American Portrait: Old Style

I

Beyond the last house, where home was,
Past the marsh we found the old skull in, all nameless
And cracked in star-shape from a stone-smack,
Up the hill where the grass was tangled waist-high and wind-tousled,
To the single great oak that, in leaf-season, hung like
A thunderhead black against whatever blue the sky had,

And here, at the widest circumference of shade, when shade was,
Ran the trench, six feet long,
And wide enough for a man to lie down in,
In comfort, if comfort was still any object. No sign there
Of any ruined cabin or well, so Pap must have died of camp fever,
And the others pushed on, God knows where.

II

The Dark and Bloody Ground, so the teacher romantically said,
But one look out the window, and woods and ruined cornfields we saw:
A careless-flung corner of country, no hope and no history here.
No hope but the Pullman lights that swept
Night-fields—glass-glint from some farmhouse and flicker of ditches—
Or the night freight's moan on the rise where
You might catch a ride on the rods,
Just for hell, or if need had arisen.
No history either—no Harrod or Finley or Boone,
No tale how the Bluebellies broke at the Rebel yell and cold steel.

So we had to invent it all, our Bloody Ground, K and I,
And him the best shot in ten counties and could call any bird-note back,
But school out, not big enough for the ballgame,

3

And in the full tide of summer, not ready
For the twelve-gauge yet, or even a job, so what
Can you do but pick up your BBs and Benjamin,
Stick corn pone in pocket, and head out
"To Rally in the Cane-Brake and Shoot the Buffalo"—
As my grandfather's cracked old voice would sing it
From days of his own grandfather—and often enough
It was only a Plymouth Rock or maybe a fat Dominecker
That fell to the crack of the unerring Decherd.

III

Yes, imagination is strong. But not strong enough in the face of
The sticky feathers and BBs a mother's hand held out.
But no liberal concern was evinced for a Redskin,
As we trailed and out-tricked the sly Shawnees
In a thicket of ironweed, and I wrestled one naked
And slick with his bear grease, till my hunting knife
Bit home, and the tomahawk
Slipped from his hand. And what mother cared about Bluebellies
Who came charging our trench? But we held
To pour the last volley at face-gape before
The tangle and clangor of bayonet.

Yes, a day is merely forever
In memory's shiningness,
And a year but a gust or a gasp
In the summer's heat of Time, and in that last summer
I was almost ready to learn
What imagination is—it is only
The lie we must learn to live by, if ever
We mean to live at all. Times change.
Things change. And K up and gone, and the summer
Gone, and I longed to know the world's name.

IV

Well, what I remember most
In a world long Time-pale and powdered
Like a vision still clinging to plaster
Set by Piero della Francesca
Is how K, through lane-dust or meadow,
Seemed never to walk, but float
With a singular joy and silence,
In his cloud of bird dogs, like angels,
With their eyes on his eyes like God,
And the sun on his uncut hair bright
As he passed through the ramshackle town and odd folks there
With pants on and vests and always soft gabble of money—
Polite in his smiling, but never much to say.

V

To pass through to what? No, not
To some wild white peak dreamed westward,
And each sunrise a promise to keep. No, only
The Big Leagues, not even a bird dog,
And girls that popped gum while they screwed.

Yes, this was his path, and no batter
Could do what booze finally did:
Just blow him off the mound—but anyway,
He had always called it a fool game, just something
For children who hadn't yet dreamed what
A man is, or barked a squirrel, or raised
A single dog from a pup.

VI

And I, too, went on my way, the winning and losing, or what
Is sometimes of all things the worst, the not knowing
One thing from the other, nor knowing
How the teeth in Time's jaw all snag backward

And whatever enters therein
Has less hope of remission than shark-meat,

And one Sunday afternoon, in the idleness of summer,
I found his farm, and him home there,
With the bird dogs crouched round in the grass
And their eyes on his eyes as he whispered
Whatever to bird dogs it was.
Then yelled: "Well, for Christ's sake—it's you!"

Yes, me, for Christ's sake, and some sixty
Years blown like a hurricane past! But what can you say—
Can you say—when *all-to-be-said* is the *done*?
So our talk ran to buffalo-hunting, and the look on his mother's face,

And the sun sank slow as he stood there,
All Indian-brown from waist up, who never liked tops to his pants,
And standing nigh straight, but the arms and the pitcher's
Great shoulders, they were thinning to old-man thin.
Sun low, all silence, then sudden:
"But, Jesus," he cried, "what makes a man do what he does—
Him living until he dies!"

Sure, all of us live till we die, but bingo!
Like young David at brookside, he swooped down,
Snatched a stone, wound up, and let fly,
And high on a pole over yonder the big brown insulator
Simply exploded. "See—I still got control!" he said.

VII

Late, late, toward sunset, I wandered
Where old dreams had once been Life's truth, and where
I saw the trench of our valor, now nothing
But a ditch full of late-season weed-growth,
Beyond the rim of shade.

*

6

There was nobody there, hence no shame to be saved from, so I
Just lie in the trench on my back and see high,
Beyond the tall ironweed stalks, or oak leaves
If I happen to look that way,
How the late summer's thinned-out sky moves,
Drifting on, drifting on, like forever,
From *where* on to *where*, and I wonder
What it would be like to die,
Like the nameless old skull in the swamp, lost,
And know yourself dead lying under
The infinite motion of sky.

VIII

But why should I lie here longer?
I am not dead yet, though in years,
And the world's way is yet long to go,
And I love the world even in my anger,
And love is a hard thing to outgrow.

Amazing Grace in the Back Country

In the season of late August star-fall,
When the first crickets crinkled the dark,
There by woods, where oaks of the old forest-time
Yet swaggered and hulked over upstarts, the tent
Had been pitched, no bigger than one of
Some half-bankrupt carnival come
To town with fat lady, human skeleton, geek,
Man-woman and moth-eaten lion, and one
Boa constrictor for two bits seen
Fed a young calf; plus a brace
Of whores to whom menopause now
Was barely a memory, one with gold teeth and one
With game gam, but both
With aperture ready to serve
Any late-lingerers, and leave
A new and guaranteed brand of syphilis handy—yes,

The tent old and yellowed and patched,
Lit inside by three wire-hung gasoline lamps
That outside, through threadbare canvas, were muted to gold.
Here no carnival now—the tabernacle
To the glory of God the Most High, for now corn
Was laid by, business slack, such business as was, and
The late-season pain gnawing deep at the human bone
As the season burned on to its end.

God's Word and His glory—and I, aged twelve,
Sat there while an ex-railroad engineer
Turned revivalist shouted the Threat and the Promise, with sweat

On his brow, and shirt plastered to belly, and
Eyes a-glaze with the mania of joy.

And now by my knees crouched some old-fool dame
In worn-out black silk, there crouching with tears
In her eyes as she tugged me to kneel
And save my pore twelve-year-old soul
Before too late. She wept.
She wept and she prayed, and I knew I was damned,
Who was guilty of all short of murder,
At least in my heart and no alibi there, and once
I had walked down a dark street, lights out in houses,
Uttering, "Lust—lust—lust,"
Like an invocation, out loud—and the word
So lovely, fresh-minted.

I saw others fall as though stricken. I heard
The shout of salvation. I stared
In the red-rimmed, wet eyes of the crazy old dame,
Whose name I never remembered, but knew
That she loved me—the Pore Little Lamb—and I thought
How old bones now creaked in God's name.

But the Pore Little Lamb, he hardened his heart,
Like a flint nigger-head rounded slick in a creek-bed
By generations of flood, and suddenly
I found myself standing, then
Ran down an aisle, and outside,
Where cool air and dark filled my lungs, and fifty
Yards off, with my brow pressed hard
On the scaly bark of a hickory tree,
Vomited. Fumbling
In darkness, I found the spring
And washed my mouth. Humped there,
       *

And knowing damnation, I stared
Through interstices of black brush to the muted gold glow
Of God's canvas, till in
The last hymn of triumph rose voices, and hearts
Burst with joy at amazing grace so freely given,
And moving on into darkness,

Voices sang of amazing grace, singing as they
Straggled back to the village, where voice after voice died away,
As singer by singer, in some dark house,
Found bed and lay down,
And tomorrow would rise and do all the old things to do,
Until that morning they would not rise, not ever.

And now, when all voices were stilled and the lamps
Long out in the tent, and stars
Had changed place in the sky, I yet lay
By the spring with one hand in the cold black water
That showed one star in reflection, alone—and lay
Wondering and wondering how many
A morning would I rise up to greet,
And what grace find.

But that was long years ago. I was twelve years old then.

Boy Wandering in Simms' Valley

Through brush and love-vine, well blooded by blackberry thorn
Long dry past prime, under summer's late molten light
And past the last rock-slide at ridge-top and stubborn,
Raw tangle of cedar, I clambered, breath short and spit white

From lung-depth. Then down the lone valley, called Simms' Valley still,
Where Simms, long back, had nursed a sick wife till she died.
Then turned out his spindly stock to forage at will,
And took down his twelve-gauge, and simply lay down by her side.

No kin they had, and nobody came just to jaw.
It was two years before some straggling hunter sat down
On the porch-edge to rest, then started to prowl. He saw
What he saw, saw no reason to linger, so high-tailed to town.

A dirt-farmer needs a good wife to keep a place trim,
So the place must have gone to wrack with his old lady sick.
And when I came there, years later, old furrows were dim,
And dimmer in fields where grew maples and such, a span thick.

So for years the farm had contracted: now barn down, and all
The yard back to wilderness gone, and only
The house to mark human hope, but ready to fall.
No buyer at tax-sale, it waited, forgotten and lonely.

I stood in the bedroom upstairs, in lowering sun,
And saw sheets hang spiderweb-rotten, and blankets a mass
Of what weather and leaves from the broken window had done,
Not to mention the rats. And thought what had there come to pass.

*

But lower was sinking the sun. I shook myself,
Flung a last glance around, then suddenly
Saw the old enameled bedpan, high on a shelf.
I stood still again, as the last sun fell on me,

And stood wondering what life is, and love, and what they may be.

Old Flame

I never then noticed the rather sausage-like trotters
That toted incomparable glory down the street
Schoolward, for glory's the only thing that matters,
That glory then being twin braids plaited plump and neat,

One over each shoulder with a bewitching twitch
To mark each pace as I followed, drifting, tongue-tied,
Gaze fixed on the sun's stunning paradox which
Gave to blackness a secret flaming that blackness denied.

Tongue-tied—why, yes. And besides, she was somewhat older,
So in nine years no word ever passed, certainly not conversation.
Then I was gone, and as far as I cared, she could moulder,
Braids and all, in the grave, life carved in compressed notation.

A half-century later, stranger on streets back home,
I heard my name, but on turning saw no one I knew.
Then I saw the mouth open and move, of a grisly old dame,
With gingham, false teeth, gray hair, and heard words: "Why, it's you!"

Well, yes, it was me, but who was that pile of age-litter?
"Don't you know me?" it wailed. Then suddenly, by Christ, I did.
So at last conversation—just factual, not joyous or bitter:
Twice widowed, grandmother, but comfortably fixed, she said,

And solstice and solstice will heave on, on its axis earth grind,
And black Cadillacs scarcely hold a funereal pace.
When her name escapes, I can usually call to mind
Sausage-legs, maybe some kind of braids. Never, never, a face.

Evening Hour

There was a graveyard once—or cemetery
It's now more toney to say—just a field without fence
Pretty far from town, on a hill good and gravelly
So rain wouldn't stand to disturb local residents,

Though all were long past the sniffles and rheumatism:
A tract of no real estate value, where flourished not
Even thistle, and the spade at the grievous chasm
Would go *chink* on chipped flint in the dirt, for in times forgot

Here the Indian crouched to perfect his arrowhead.
And there was a boy, long after, who gathered such things
Among shiny new tombstones recording the first-planted dead,
Now and then looking up at a buzzard's high sun-glinting wings,

Not thinking of flesh and its nature, but suddenly still
For maybe two minutes; as when, up the rise, a great through-freight
Strove in the panting and clank of man's living will,
Asserting itself in the face of an ignorant date.

Not morbid, nor putting two and two together
To make any mystic, or fumblingly philosophical,
Four, he sometimes kept waiting, if decent the weather,
In a lonely way, arrowheads forgotten, till all

The lights of the town had come on. He did not know
Why the lights, so familiar, now seemed so far away,
And more than once felt the crazy impulse grow
To lay ear to earth for what voices beneath might say.

Orphanage Boy

From the orphanage Al came to
Work on the farm as what you'd call
Hired boy if he got enough to
Call hire. Back at the woodpile chop-
ping stove-lengths, he taught me all the
Dirty words I'd never heard of
Or learned from farm observation,
And generally explained how
Folks went in for fun, adding that
A farm was one hell of a place
For finding fun.

           Polite enough,
He'd excuse himself after sup-
per and go sit on the stile with
Bob, the big white farm bulldog, close
At his side, and watch the sun sink
Back of the barn or, maybe in
The opposite direction, the
Moon rise.

          It was a copperhead
Bit Bob, and nothing, it looked like,
Would make him better. Just after
Supper one night my uncle stood
On the front porch and handed a
Twelve-gauge to Al, and said, "Be sure
You do it right back of the head."
He never named Bob's name.
    *

                    Al's face
Was white as clabber, but he took
The gun, not saying a word, just
Walking away down the lane to-
ward sunset, Bob too, me follow-
ing. Then, in the woods where it was
Nigh dark, he did it. He gave me
The gun, smoke still in the muzzle,
Said, "Git away, you son-a-bitch,"
And I got away and he lay
On the dead leaves crying even
Before I was gone.

              That night he
Never came home and the Sheriff
Never found him.

              It was six months
Before I went back in the woods
To the place. There was a real grave
There. There was a wood cross on the
Grave. He must have come back to the
Barn for the shovel and hammer,
And back again to hang them up.

It must have taken nigh moonset.

Red-Tail Hawk and Pyre of Youth

TO HAROLD BLOOM

1

Breath clamber-short, face sun-peeled, stones
Loose like untruth underfoot, I
Had just made the ridge crest, and there,
Opening like joy, the unapprehensible purity
Of afternoon flooded, in silver,
The sky. It was
The hour of stainless silver just before
The gold begins.

Eyes, strangely heavy like lead,
Drew down to the .30-30 hung on my hand
As on a crooked stick, in growing wonder
At what it might really be. It was as though
I did not know its name. Nor mine. Nor yet had known
That all is only
All, and part of all. No wind
Moved the silver light. No movement,

Except for the center of
That convex perfection, not yet
A dot even, nameless, no color, merely
A shadowy vortex of silver. Then,
In widening circles—oh, nearer!
And suddenly I knew the name, and saw,
As though seeing, coming toward me,
Unforgiving, the hot blood of the air:
Gold eyes, unforgiving, for they, like God, see all.

2

There was no decision in the act,
There was no choice in the act—the act impossible but
Possible. I screamed, not knowing
From what emotion, as at that insane range
I pressed the cool, snubbed
Trigger. Saw
The circle
Break.

3

Heart leaping in joy past definition, in
Eyes tears past definition, by rocky hill and valley
Already dark-devoured, the bloody
Body already to my bare flesh embraced, cuddled
Like babe to heart, and my heart beating like love:
Thus homeward.

But nobody there.

So at last
I dared stare in the face—the lower beak drooping,
As though from thirst, eyes filmed.
Like a secret, I wrapped it in newspaper quickly
And hid it deep
In the ice chest.

Too late to start now.

4

Up early next morning, with
My father's old razor laid out, the scissors,
Pliers and needles, waxed thread,
The burlap and salt, the arsenic and clay,
Steel rods, thin, and glass eyes

Gleaming yellow. Oh, yes,
I knew my business. And at last a red-tail—

Oh, king of the air!

And at that miraculous range.

How my heart sang!

Till all was ready—skull now well scraped
And with arsenic dried, and all flesh joints, and the cape
Like a carapace feathered in bronze, and naturally anchored
At beak and at bone joints, and steel
Driven through to sustain wing and bone
And the clay-burlap body built there within.
It was molded as though for that moment to take to the air—though,
In God's truth, the chunk of poor wingless red meat,
The model from which all was molded, lay now
Forever earthbound, fit only
For dog tooth, not sky.

5
Year after year, in my room, on the tallest of bookshelves,
It was regal, perched on its bough-crotch to guard
Blake and *Lycidas*, Augustine, Hardy and *Hamlet*,
Baudelaire and Rimbaud, and I knew that the yellow eyes,
Unsleeping, stared as I slept.

Till I slept in that room no more.

6
Years pass like a dream, are a dream, and time came
When my mother was dead, father bankrupt, and whiskey
Hot in my throat while there for the last
*

Time I lay, and my heart
Throbbed slow in the
Meaningless motion of life, and with
Eyes closed I knew
That yellow eyes somewhere, unblinking, in vengeance stared.

Or *was* it vengeance? What could I know?

Could Nature forgive, like God?

7

That night in the lumber room, late,
I found him—the hawk, feathers shabby, one
Wing bandy-banged, one foot gone sadly
Askew, one eye long gone—and I reckoned
I knew how it felt with one gone.

And all relevant items I found there: my first book of Milton,
The *Hamlet*, the yellow, leaf-dropping Rimbaud, and a book
Of poems friends and I had printed in college, not to mention
The collection of sexual Japanese prints—strange sex
Of mechanical sexlessness. And so made a pyre for
The hawk that, though gasoline-doused and wing-dragging,
Awaited, with what looked like pride,
The match.

8

Flame flared. Feathers first, and I flinched, then stood
As the steel wire warped red to defend
The shape designed godly for air. But
It fell with the mass, and I
Did not wait.

What left
To do but walk in the dark, and no stars?

9

Some dreams come true, some no.
But I've waked in the night to see
High in the late and uncurdled silver of summer
The pale vortex appear once again—and you come
And always the rifle swings up, though with
The weightlessness now of dream,
The old .30-30 that knows
How to bind us in air-blood and earth-blood together
In our commensurate fate,
Whose name is a name beyond joy.

10

And I pray that in some last dream or delusion,
While hospital wheels creak beneath
And the nurse's soles make their *squeak-squeak* like mice,
I'll again see the first small silvery swirl
Spin outward and downward from sky-height
To bring me the truth in blood-marriage of earth and air—
And all will be as it was
In that paradox of unjoyful joyousness,
Till the dazzling moment when I, a last time, must flinch
From the regally feathered gasoline flare
Of youth's poor, angry, slapdash, and ignorant pyre.

Mountain Plateau

TO JAMES WRIGHT

At the center of acres of snow-whiteness
The snag-oak reared, black and old, boughs
Crank. Topmost twigs—pen-strokes, tangle, or stub—fretted
The ice-blue of sky. A crow,
On the highest black, frail, and sky-thrust support,

Uttered

Its cry to the immense distance.

I hear the cry across the immense distance
Of the landscape of my heart.

That landscape now reduplicates, snow-white, the one
In which I once stood. At its center, too, the
Black snag stands.

A crow gleams there up-thrust against the blue sky.

I can make no answer
To the cry from the immense distance,

My eyes fill with tears. I have lived
Long without being able
To make adequate communication.

Star-Fall

In that far land, and time, near the castrated drawbridge where
For four bloody centuries garbage
In the moat's depth had been spilled
To stink, but most at the broiling noontide—
There we, now at midnight, lay.

We lay on the dry grass of August, high
On our cliff, and the odor we caught was of bruised
Rosemary at pathside, not garbage, and sometimes
The salt air of sea, and the only sound to our ears
Was the slap and hiss far below, for the sea has never forgiven
The nature of stone.

We did not lie close, and for hours
The only contact was fingers, and motionless they.
For what communication
Is needed if each alone
Is sunk and absorbed into
The mass and matrix of Being that defines
Identity of all?

We lay in the moonless night,
Felt earth beneath us swing,
Watched the falling stars of the season. They fell
Like sparks in a shadowy, huge smithy, with
The clang of the hammer unheard.

Far off in the sea's matching midnight,
The fishing lights marked their unfabled constellations.
                 *

We found nothing to say, for what can a voice say when
The world is a voice, no ear needing?

We lay watching the stars as they fell.

Youth Stares at Minoan Sunset

On the lap of the mountain meadow,
At the break of the cliff-quarry where
Venetians had once sawed their stone, soft
Nag of surf far below foot, he
Stares seaward the distance to sunset.

The sky is rose-hearted, immense, undisturbed.
In that light the youth's form is black, without motion,
And birds, gull nor other, have no transaction
In the inflamed emptiness of sky. Mountainward,
No bird cries. We had called once,
But we were too far, too far.

Molten and massy, of its own weight flattened,
The sun accelerates downward, the sea,
From general slate-blue, flaming upward.
Contact is made at the horizon-line.

On that line, one instant, one only,
The great coin, flame-massy and with
The frail human figure thereon minted black,
Balances. Suddenly is gone. A gull
Defiles at last the emptiness of air.

We are closer now. The black
Silhouette, yet small, stares seaward. To our cry
It does not turn. Later,
It will, and turning, see us with a slow

And pitying happiness of recognition born of
A knowledge we do not yet have. Or have forgotten.

He spreads his arms to the sky as though he loves it—and us.

He is so young.

II
SPECULATIVE

Dream

Waters, hypnotic, long after moonset, murmur
Under your window, and Time
Is only a shade on the underside of the beech-leaf
Which, upward, reflects a tiny refulgence of stars.

What can you dream to make Time real again?
I have read in a book that dream is the mother of memory,
And if there's no memory where—oh, what—is Time?

So grapple your dream! Like Odysseus the Cunning, who leaped
On the mountainous Ajax, and snug in that lethal embrace, while
Heels slashed at soft knee-backs, rode
Downward the great crash that
Bounced the head of the victim on hard ground, and
Jarred teeth from jawbone, and blood filled
That mouth from its tongue, like a grape-cluster, crushed.

Yes, grapple—or else the Morning Star
Westward will pale, and leave
Your ghost without history even, to wander
A desert trackless in sun-glare.

For the dream is only a self of yourself—and Jacob
Once wrestled, nightlong, his angel and, though
With wrenched thigh, had blackmailed a blessing, by dawn.

Dream of a Dream

Moonlight stumbles with bright heel
In the stream, and the stones sing.
What they sing is nothing, nothing,
But the joy Time plies to feel
In fraternal flux and glimmer
With the stream that does not know
Its destination and knows no
Truth but its own moonlit shimmer.
In my dream Time and water interflow,
And bubbles of consciousness glimmer ghostly as they go.

Tell me, tell me, whence came
That stream that sings its un-Timed song.
Tell me, as I lie here nightlong,
And listen and wonder whence my name
Bubbled forth on a moonlit stream
To glitter by the singing stone
A moment before, whirling, it is gone
Into the braiding texture of dream.
In what dark night of history, tell me what moon
Defines the glimmer and froth of self before it is gone.

From what dream to what dream do we
Awake when the first bird stirs to declare
Its glimmering dream of the golden air,
Of green and of dapple?—till finally,
From the twilight spruce thicket, darkening and far,
A thrush, sanctifying the hour, will utter

The glory of diminution. Later,
The owl's icy question shudders the air.
By this time the moonlight's bright heel has splashed the stream;
But this, of course, belongs to the dream of another dream.

First Dawn Light

By lines fainter gray than the faintest geometry
Of chalk, on a wall like a blackboard, day's first light
Defines the window edges. Last dream, last owl-cry
Now past, now is the true emptiness of night,

For not yet first bird-stir, first bird-note, only
Your breath as you wonder what daylight will bring, and you try
To recall what the last dream was, and think how lonely
In sun-blaze you have seen the buzzard hang black in the sky.

For day has its loneliness too, you think even as
First bird-stir does come, first twitter, faithless and fearful
That new night, in the deep leaves, may lurk. So silence has
Returned. Then, sudden, the glory, heart-full and ear-full,

For triggered now is the mysterious mechanism
Of the forest's joy, by temperature or by beam,
And until a sludge-thumb smears the sunset's prism,
You must wait to resume, in night's black hood, the reality of dream.

Ah, Anima!

Watch the great bough lashed by wind and rain. Is it
A metaphor for your soul—or Man's—or even

Mine in the hurricane of Time? Now,
In the gray and splintered light, in the scything

Tail of the hurricane, miles of forest around us
Heave like the sea, and the gray underside of leaf is exposed

Of every tree, non-coniferous. The tall
Pines blackly stagger. Beyond,

The bulk and backdrop of mountain is
Obscured. Can you locate yourself

On the great chart of history?
In the distance a tree crashes.

Empires have fallen, and the stream
Gnashes its teeth with the *klang* of boulders.

Later, sleep. Tomorrow, help
Will come. The Governor promises. Roads will be rebuilt,

And houses. Food distributed. But, meanwhile, sleep
Is a disaster area, too. You have lain down

In the shards of Time and the un-roar of the wind of being,
And when, in the dark, you wake, with only
   *

The *klang* of distant boulders in your ears,
You may wish that you, even in the wrack and pelt of gray light,

Had run forth, screaming as wind snatched your breath away
Until you were nameless—oh, anima!—and only

Your mouth, rounded, is there, the utterance gone. Perhaps
That is the only purity—to leave

The husk behind, and leap
Into the blind and antiseptic anger of air.

Unless

All will be in vain unless—unless what? Unless
You realize that what you think is Truth is only

A husk for something else. Which might,
Shall we say, be called energy, as good a word as any. As when

The rattlesnake, among desert rocks
And Freudian cactus tall in moonlight,

Scrapes off the old integument, and flows away,
Clean and lethal and gleaming like water over moon-bright sand,

Unhusked for its mission. Oh, *neo nato!* fanged, unforgiving,
We worship you. In the morning,

In the ferocity of daylight, the old skin
Will be translucent and abstract, like Truth. The mountains,

In distance, will glitter like diamonds, or salt.
They too will, in that light, seem abstract.

At night I have stood there, and the wide world
Was flat and circular under the storm of the

Geometry of stars. The mountains, in starlight, were black
And black-toothed to define the enormous circle

Of desert of which I was the center. This
Is one way to approach the question.
　　*

All is in vain unless you can, motionless, standing there,
Breathe with the rhythm of stars.

You cannot, of course, see your own face, but you know that it,
Lifted, is stripped to white bone by starlight. This is happening.

This is happiness.

Not Quite Like a Top

Did you know that the earth, not like a top on its point,
Spins on an axis that sways, and swings, from its middle?

Well, I didn't know, but do now, and often at night,
After maybe three highballs, I lie in my bed,

In the dark, and try to feel the off-center sensation,
And sometimes if

(In the northern hemisphere, this) my head points north,
I do. Or maybe I do. It is like

So many things they say are true, but you
Can't always be sure you feel them,

Even in dark, in bed, head north.
I have, in shameless dark, sometimes

Wept because
I couldn't be sure something precious was true,

Like they say. Examples could be multiplied. But
Once, in a Pullman berth (upper), I desperately prayed

To God to exist so that I
Might have the exalted horror of denying

Him. But nothing
Came of that project. Nothing. Oh, nothing.
        *

But so young was I then! And maybe the axis of earth
Does not really sway from its center, even if

Ancient Egyptian and modern astronomers say so,
And what good would it do me to have firsthand evidence,

When there's so much that I, lying in darkness, don't know?

Waiting

You will have to wait. Until it. Until
The last owl hoot has quivered to a

Vibrant silence and you realize that there is no breathing
Beside you, and dark curdles toward dawn of no dawn. Until

Drouth breaks, too late to save the corn,
But not too late for flood, and the hobbled cow, stranded

On a sudden islet, gargles in grief in the alder-brake. Until
The doctor enters the waiting room, and

His expression betrays all, and you wish
He'd take his goddam hand off your shoulder. Until

The woman you have lived with all the years
Says, without rancor, that life is the way life is, and she cannot

Remember when last she loved you, and had lived the lie only
For the children's sake. Until you become uncertain of French

Irregular verbs, and by a strange coincidence begin to take Catholic
Instruction from Monsignor O'Malley, who chews a hangnail. Until

You realize, to your surprise, that our Savior died for us all,
And as tears gather in your eyes, you burst out laughing,

For the joke is certainly on Him, considering
What we are. Until
  *

You pick the last alibi off, like a scab, and
Admire the inwardness, as beautiful as inflamed

Flesh, or summer sunrise. Until
You remember that, remarkably, common men have done noble deeds. Until

It grows on you that, at least, God
Has allowed man the grandeur of certain utterances.

True or not. But sometimes true.

The Mission

In the dark kitchen the electric icebox rustles.
It whispers like the interior monologue of guilt and extenuation,
And I wake from a dream of horses. They do not know
I am dreaming of them. By this time they must be long dead.

Behind barbed wire, in fog off the sea, they stand.
Two clumps of horses, uncavorting, like gray stone, stand,
Heavy manes unrustling in the gray sea wind.
The sea is gray. Night falls. Later, the manes will rustle,

But ever so little, in wind lifting off the Bay of Biscay. But no—
They are dead. *La boucherie chevaline*, in the village,
Has a gold horse-head above the door. I wake
From my dream, and know that the shadow

Of the great spruce close by my house must be falling
Black on the white roof of winter. The spruce
Wants to hide the house from the moon, for
The moon's intentions have never been quite clear.

The spruce does not know that a square of moonlight lies cunningly on
The floor by my bed, and I watch it and think how,
On the snow-locked mountain, deep in a fissure
Under the granite ledge, the bear

Huddles inside his fur like an invalid inside
A charity-ward blanket. Fat has thinned on bone, and the fur
Is too big for him now. He stirs in sleep, farts
Gently in the glacial blackness of the cave. The eyes
            *

Do not open. Outside, in moonlight,
The ledges are bearded with ice, and the brook,
Black, crawls under ice. It has a mission, but,
In that blackness, has forgotten what. I, too,

Have forgotten the nature of my own mission. This
May be fortunate, for if I stare at the dark ceiling
And try to remember, I do not have to go back to sleep,
And not sleeping, will not again dream

Of clumps of horses, fog-colored in sea fog, rumps
To the sea wind, standing like stone primitively hewn,
While the fields, gray, stretch beyond them, and distance dies.
Perhaps that lost mission is to try to understand

The possibility of joy in the world's tangled and hieroglyphic beauty.

Code Book Lost

What does the veery say, at dusk in shad-thicket?
There must be some meaning, or why should your heart stop,

As though, in the dark depth of water, Time held its breath,
While the message spins on like a spool of silk thread fallen?

When white breakers lunge at the black basalt cliff, what
Does the heart hear, gale lifting, the last star long gone now,

Or what in the mother's voice calling her boy from the orchard,
In a twilight moth-white with the apple blossom's dispersal?

Yes, what is that undeclared timbre, and why
Do your eyes go moist, and a pain of unworthiness strike?

What does the woman dying, or supine and penetrated, stare at?
Fly on ceiling, or gold mote afloat in a sun-slit of curtains?

Some message comes thus from a world that screams, far off.
Will she understand before what will happen, will happen?

What meaning, when at the unexpected street corner,
You meet some hope long forgotten, and your old heart,

Like neon in shore-fog, or distance, glows dimly again?
Will you waver, or clench stoic teeth and move on?
　　*

Have you thought as you walk, late, late, the streets of a town
Of all dreams being dreamed in dark houses? What do they signify?

Yes, message on message, like wind or water, in light or in dark,
The whole world pours at us. But the code book, somehow, is lost.

When the Tooth Cracks—Zing!

When the tooth cracks—zing!—it
Is like falling in love, or like
Remembering your mother's face when she—and you only
A child—smiled, or like
Falling into Truth. This,
Of course, before the pain
Begins. But even
The pain is something—is, you might say,
For lack of a better word,
Reality.

      Do you
Remember that Jacob Boehme saw
Sunlight flash on a pewter platter on
The table, and his life was totally changed?

Is the name of God nothing more than
The accidental flash on a platter? But what is accident?

I have waked in the dark with the heart-throbbing conviction
Of having just seen some masterly
Shape, but without name. The world
Is suddenly different, then
The pain begins. Sharp as a snapped tooth, it strikes.
And, again, I have waked knowing
That I have only been dreaming,
In classic and timeless precision, of
Winter moonlight flooding a large room where
No spark now winks on the hearth, a broken
Brandy snifter glitters in moonshine by the coffee table, a

Half-burned cigarette butt beside it. And
A woman's slipper lies on its side
On the moon-bleached rug. In moonshine,
Silky as pastel, dust covers all.

It is only a dream, but it must have a name.
Must we totally forget a thing to know it?
Perhaps redemption is nothing more than the way
We learn to live with memories that are no longer remembered.

But it is hard to know the end of a story.

We often pray God to let us have Truth.
It is more important to pray God to help us to live with it.

Especially if your memory is not what it used to be.

Sister Water

. . . and to begin again, the night was dark and dreary, and
The Captain said to his trusty Lieutenant, "Lieutenant,

Tell us a story." And the Lieutenant: "The night was dark and—" And I
Have heard on the creaky stairs at night an old man's

Dragging step approach my door. He pauses for breath, and I
Can hear the chain-rattle of phlegm in the painful intake,

But I never know whose father it is, or son,
Or what mission leads to my locked door. If I

Should open it, he might call me by my name. Or yours.
And if he did, then what, what might occur?

And once, not knowing where, in what room, in what city even,
You lay in the dark, and a finger,

Soft as down and with a scent
Unidentifiable but stirring your heart to tears,

Like memory, was laid to your lips. "Now—"
Comes the whisper. But is there a *now* or a *then*?

And you hear in the dark, at street level above
Your basement apartment window, tires hiss on wet asphalt.

You do not know whence they come, nor whither go,
And so lie laughing alone with a sound like a strangled loon-call,
        *

Till, slop-gray, dawn light defines the bars of your window,
And you hear the cough and mastication of

The garbage truck in the next block. "God—"
You think, with a stab of joy, "He loves us all. He will not

Let all distinction perish." You cannot pray. But
You can wash your face in cold water.

Memory Forgotten

Forget! Forget it to know it. It sings!
But it is too true to sing its name. Afar,

In a thicket, it sings like
Some unidentified warbler. No, don't move.

If you break a twig, it may stop. But now!—
Oh, light, elate, more liquid than thrush,

It sings. How beautiful it is!—
Now that it is only a memory

Without a name. A shadow of happiness—yes. Did you ever
Wake up at dawn, heart singing, and run out

Barefoot in the dew, and dew blazed like diamonds of light?
Or was it a kiss on the brow, the brush of a feather,

Just as you fell asleep? How long
Has your mother been dead? Or did you, much older,

Lie in the tall grass and, motionless, watch
The single white fleck of cloud forever crossing the blue—

As you lay in the summer's gilt aesthetic thralled?
How much do we forget that is ourselves—
    *

Nothing too small to make a difference,
And in the forgetting to make it all more true?

That liquid note from the thicket afar—oh, hear!
What is it you cannot remember that is so true?

Waking to Tap of Hammer

Waking up in my curtain-dark bedroom, I hear,
Cottoned in distance, the tap of a hammer:
Tap-tap. Silence. Then anguish
Of bandsaw on white oak. Yes,
I know what it is. My boy, this early
At his five-tonner at work, the schooner.
I shut eyes and see, rising upright in stocks,
The sanded gray hull. Dew-gleaming,
It swims in the first light. Yearns long Atlanticward.

He lives in a dream of his passion, hands
Never quite still, eyes often fixed on great distance.
You speak, and he seems not to hear. Slowly, then smiles.
He sleeps while the blue prints stare down in the darkness.
Tools gleam when a star spies in.
His head is thrown back in sleep. He dreams
Of sail-crack like a pistol, of spume.
Gulls scream in their hypothetical sky.

Oh, tell me the nature of passion and the fruit thereof!
What would I have otherwise than this truth, even my own dream?
Who have waked in the night from a dream
In which I, like a spirit, hung in the squall-heart—
There saw how, one rag of a spitfire jib forward, the bows
Clambered gray wave-steep, plunged, and emerged,
While through rain-slash and spray-roil,
Behind plexiglass dome, hands on wheel, the face,
Carven, stared forth: gannet-gaze, osprey-eye. Slowly, it smiled.

I dreamed it was smiling at me.

Love Recognized

There are many things in the world and you
Are one of them. Many things keep happening and
You are one of them, and the happening that
Is you keeps falling like snow
On the landscape of not-you, hiding hideousness, until
The streets and the world of wrath are choked with snow.

How many things have become silent? Traffic
Is throttled. The mayor
Has been, clearly, remiss, and the city
Was totally unprepared for such a crisis. Nor
Was I—yes, why should this happen to me?
I have always been a law-abiding citizen.

But you, like snow, like love, keep falling,

And it is not certain that the world will not be
Covered in a glitter of crystalline whiteness.

Silence.

The Smile

Mellow, mellow, at thrush-hour
Swells the note to redeem all—
Sweat and swink and daytime's rancor,
And the thought that all's not worth all.

Blue in distance while the sun dips,
Talus, cliff, and forest melt
Into the promise that soon sleep
Will heal the soul's identity.

If a hand is laid to a hand now,
Hard to soft, or soft to hard,
Can that contact stir the dream,
Long light-lost, of an un-selfed joy?

Yes, perhaps—but remember
Dreams in devious orders thrive.
Nightmare may nook in any bosom,
And saint or mother, in darkness, make outcry.

Nevertheless, our hands have met now
As heels on the darkening gravel grind,
And, star by star, the purpled sky
Defines the season's constellations.

What will come will come, and dawn
May breed a dream we may dream real:
Your hand-back, task-tired, pushes up
Damp hair to show the flickering smile.

How to Tell a Love Story

There is a story that I must tell, but
The feeling in my chest is too tight, and innocence
Crawls through the tangles of fear, leaving,
Dry and translucent, only its old skin behind like
A garter snake's annual discard in the ground juniper. If only

I could say just the first word with breath
As sweet as a babe's and with no history—but, Christ,
If there is no history there is no story.
And no Time, no word.
For then there is nothing for a word to be about, a word

Being frozen Time only, and I have dived deep
Where light faded from gold to dark blue, and darker below,
And my chest was filled with a story like innocence,
But I rose, rose up, and plunged into light-blaze brutal as blackness,
And the sky whirled like fireworks. Perhaps I could then have begun it.

If only the first word would come and untwist my tongue!
Then the story might grow like Truth, or a tree, and your face
Would lean at me. If only the story could begin when Time truly began,
White surf and a storm of sunlight, you running ahead and a smile
Back-flung—but then, how go cn? For what would it mean?

Perhaps I can't say the first word till I know what it all means.
Perhaps I can't know till finally the doctor comes in and leans.

Little Black Heart of the Telephone

That telephone keeps screaming its little black heart out:
Nobody there? Oh, nobody's there!—and the blank room bleeds
For the poor little black bleeding heart of the telephone.
I, too, have suffered. I know how it feels
When you scream and scream, and nobody's there.
I am feeling that way this goddam minute,
If for no particular reason.

Tell the goddam thing to shut up! Only
It's not ringing now at all, but I
Can scrutinize it and tell that it's thinking about
Ringing, and just any minute, I know.
So, you demand, *the room's not empty, you're there?*
Yes, I'm here, but it might start screaming just after
I've gone out the door, in my private silence.

Or if I stayed here I mightn't answer, might pretend
Not to be here at all, or just be part of the blankness
The room is, as the blankness
Bleeds for the little bleeding black heart
Of the telephone. If, in fact, it should scream,
My heart would bleed too, for I know how pain can't find words.
Or sometimes is afraid to find them.

I tell you because I know you will understand.
I know you have screamed: *Nobody there? Oh, nobody's there!*
You've looked up at stars lost in blankness that bleeds
Its metaphysical blood, but not of redemption.
Have you ever stopped by the roadside at night, and couldn't
Remember your name, and breath

Came short? Or at night waked up with a telephone screaming,
And covered your head, afraid to answer?

Anyway, in broad daylight, I'm now in the street,
And no telephone anywhere near, or even
Thinking about me. But tonight, back in bed, I may dream
Of a telephone screaming its little black heart out,
In an empty room, toward sunset,
While a year-old newspaper, yellowing, lies on the floor, and velvety
Dust thick over everything, especially
On the black telephone, on which no thumb-print has,
For a long time now, been visible.

In my dream I wonder why, long since, it's not been disconnected.

Last Laugh

The little Sam Clemens, one night back in Hannibal,
Peeped through the dining-room keyhole, to see, outspread
And naked, the father split open, lights, liver, and all
Spilling out from that sack of mysterious pain, and the head

Sawed through, where his Word, like God's, held its deepest den,
And candlelight glimmered on blood-slick, post-mortem steel,
And the two dead fish-eyes stared steadily ceilingward—well, then,
If you yourself were, say, twelve, just how would you feel?

Oh, not that you'd loved him—that ramrod son of Virginia,
Though born for success, failing westward bitterly on.
"Armed truce"—that was all, years later, you could find to say in you.
But still, when a father's dead, an umbrella's gone

From between the son and the direful elements.
No, Sam couldn't turn from the keyhole. It's not every night
You can see God butchered in such learned dismemberments,
And when the chance comes you should make the most of the sight.

Though making the most, Sam couldn't make terms with the fact
Of the strangely prismatic glitter that grew in his eye,
Or climbing the stairs, why his will felt detached from the act,
Or why stripping for bed, he stared so nakedly

At the pore little body and thought of the slick things therein.
Then he wept on the pillow, surprised at what he thought grief,
Then fixed eyes at darkness while, slow, on his face grew a grin,
Till suddenly something inside him burst with relief,

*

Like a hog-bladder blown up to bust when the hog-killing frost
Makes the brats' holiday. So took then to laughing and could not
Stop, and so laughed himself crying to sleep. At last,
Far off in Nevada, by campfire or sluice or gulch-hut,

Or in roaring S.F., in an acre of mirror and gilt,
Where the boys with the dust bellied-up, he'd find words come,
His own face stiff as a shingle, and him little-built.
Then whammo!—the back-slapping riot. He'd stand, looking dumb.

God was dead, for a fact. He knew, in short, the best joke.
He had learned its thousand forms, and since the dark stair-hall
Had learned what was worth more than bullion or gold-dust-plump poke.
And married rich, too, with an extra spin to the ball;

For Livy loved God, and he'd show her the joke, how they lied.
Quite a tussle it was, but hot deck or cold, he was sly
And won every hand but the last. Then at her bedside
He watched dying eyes stare up at a comfortless sky,

And was left alone with his joke, God dead, till he died.

Heat Lightning

Heat lightning prowls, pranks the mountain horizon like
Memory. I follow the soundless flicker,

As ridge after ridge, as outline of peak after peak,
Is momentarily defined in the

Pale wash, the rose-flush, of distance. Somewhere—
Somewhere far beyond them—that distance. I think

Of the past and how this soundlessness, no thunder,
Is like memory purged of emotion,

Or even of meaning. I watch
The lightning wash pale beyond the night mountains, beyond

Night cumulus, like a stage set. Nothing
Is real, and I think of her, in timelessness: the clutch

In the lightless foyer, the awkward wall-propping, one ear
Cocked for footsteps, all the world

Hates a lover. It seems only a dream, the unsounding
Flicker of memory, even the episode when

Arms, encircling, had clamped arms to sides, the business
Banked on a pillow, head

Back over bed-edge, the small cry of protest—
But meanwhile, paradoxically, heels

*

Beating buttocks in deeper demand. Then heels stopping
In shudder and sprawl, only whites

Of eyes showing, like death. What all the tension,
The tingle, twist, tangle, the panting and pain,

What all exploitation of orifices and bruised flesh but
The striving for one death in two? I remember—

Oh, look! in that flash, how the peak
Blackens zenithward—as I said, I remember

The glutted, slack look on the face once
And the faintest blood-smear at the mouth's left corner,

And not till next day did I notice the two
Symmetrical half-moons of blue marks tattooed

On my shoulder, not remembering, even then, the sensation
Of the event; and of course, not now, for heat lightning

Is thunderless. And thunderless, even,
The newspaper obit, years later, I stumbled on. Yes,

How faint that flash! And I sit in the unmooned
Dark of an August night, waiting to see

The rose-flush beyond the black peaks, and think how far,
Far away, down what deep valley, scree, scar,

The thunder redoubled, redoubling, rolls. Here silence.

Inevitable Frontier

Be careful! Slow and careful, for you now approach
The frontier where the password is difficult to utter—or grasp.

Echo among chert peaks and perilously balanced boulders
Has something to do with it, not to mention your early rearing, with

Its naïve logic. For remember now, this is the frontier
Where words coming out of a mouth are always upside-

Down, and all tongues are sloppily cubical, and shadows of nothing are,
Whatever the hour, always something, and tend to bleed

If stepped on—oh, do keep mindful how
Slick the blood of shadow can be, especially

If the shadow is of nothing. As a corollary,
The shadow of something, yourself for instance,

Provides its own peculiar hazards. You may trip
On it, and start falling upward, screaming,

Screaming for somebody to grab you before you are out
Of reach. Your eyes, too, must be readjusted, for

Here people, owl-like, see only by dark, and grope by day. Here,
People eat in shamefaced privacy, but the great Public Square,

Sparsely planted, is full, in daylight, of gut-wheeze and littered with feces
Till the carts come, and later, *à l'heure sexuelle*, at noon, waiters wheel out

*

61

To the café terraces divans of ingeniously provocative designs,
While clients, now clad in filmy robes, emerge from locker-rooms, laughing

Like children at tag. Food is, of course, forbidden, but scented drinks,
And coffee, are served under awnings. Another item:

Criminality is rare, but those convicted,
Mystically deprived of the memory of their names, are exiled

To the Isles of the Blest, where they usually end by swallowing their tongues,
This from boredom, for in their language *bliss* and *boredom*

Have the same linguistic root. Yes, many things
Are different here, and to be happy and well-adjusted, you

Must put out of mind much you have been taught. Among others, the names
Of Plato, St. Paul, Spinoza, Pascal and Freud must not be spoken, and when,

Without warning, by day or night, the appalling
White blaze of God's Great Eye sweeps the sky, History

Turns tail and scuttles back to its burrow
Like a groundhog caught in a speeding sportscar's headlight.

Heart of the Backlog

Snug at hearthside, while heart of the backlog
Of oak simmers red in the living pulse of its own
Decay, you sit. You count
Your own heartbeat. How steady, how
Firm! What, ah, is Time! And sometimes

It is hard, after all, to decide
If the ticking you now hear is
A whisk of granules of snow,
Hard and belated on panes, or simply
The old organ, fist-size and resolute,
Now beastlike caught
In your rib-cage, to pace

But go nowhere. It does,
In a ghostly sense, suggest now the sound of
Pacing, as if, in soft litter, curved claws
Were muffled. Or is it
The pace of the muffled old clock in the hall?

You watch the talus-like slide of
Consumed oak from oak yet consuming. Yes, tell me
How many the years that burn there. How delicate, dove-gray
The oak-ash that, tiny and talus-like, slides to unwink
The glowing of oak and the years unconsumed!
What is the color of years your fireplace consumes as you sit there?

But think, shut your eyes. Shut your eyes and see only
The wide stretch of world beyond your warm refuge—fields
Windless and white in full moonlight,

Snow past and now steady the stars, and, far off,
The woods-lair of darkness. Listen! is that
The great owl that you, warm at your hearthside, had heard?

How feather-frail, think, is the track of the vole
On new snow! How wide is the world! How fleeting and thin
Its mark of identity, breath
In a minuscule issue of whiteness
In air that is brighter than steel! The vole pauses, one paw
Uplifted in whiteness of moonlight.

There is no indication of what angle, or slant,
The great shadow may silkily accent the beauty of snow,
And the vole, Little One, has neither theology nor
Aesthetic—not even what you may call
Stoicism, as when the diagnostician pauses, and coughs.
Poor thing, he has only himself. And what do you have

When you go to the door, snatch it open, and, cold,
The air strikes like steel down your lungs, and you feel
The Pascalian nausea make dizzy the last stars?
Then shut the door. The backlog burns down. You sit and

Again the owl calls, and with some sadness you wonder
If at last, when the air-scything shadow descends
And needles claw-clamp through gut, heart and brain,
Will ecstasy melting with terror create the last little cry?
Is God's love but the last and most mysterious word for death?

Has the thought ever struck you to rise and go forth—yes, lost
In the whiteness—to never look upward, or back, only on,
And no sound but the snow-crunch, and breath
Gone crisp like the crumpling of paper? Listen!
Could that be the creak of a wing-joint gigantic in distance?
    *

No, no—just a tree, far off, when ice inward bites.
No, no, don't look back—oh, I beg you!

I beg you not to look back, in God's name.

Identity and Argument for Prayer

Having been in this place, I will leave it—
For good and all, I said. In Space: as legs make motion
Like scissors, motors spin, planes
Eat sky with roar gradually diminishing
To silence. In Time:
Like a self-winding watch that
Falls forever in black Spacelessness
Beyond the last stars.
This much I said.
And did. How long ago!

How is it that I am *there* again?
Space and Time our arbitrary illusions: even so,
How odd that my feet fit old foot-tracks, crushing,
Freshly again, the fresh sea-rose, imprinting
The same sea-sand while surf, heaving
At volcanic stone, black, utters
The same old prophecy, which
I knew could never come true. But it did—or did it?
I could never be sure,
But I'm *there*, now again!
Was that what the prophecy said?
Against all sense,
And will?

Thus I stand again making new the old tracks
My tennis shoes made years back, and now,
Astonished, I see that I, this instant, wear old tennis shoes,
And in the same instant become aware of
Old hope, old pain, old evil, old good,

All long forgotten, and
Do not know more than the maple by my window
On which green leaves expand in silence
To unwittingly dream of fall-redness,
As though I had dreamed all the years
This dream of return.
If that is truly what it is.

Yes, I once stood there, and now have
Just dreamed, in painful vividness, of standing
Again *there*, but if
I should, I have it on good authority, that
There is not there any more,
Having dropped through Time into otherness.
But what did happen *there* is—just now
In its new ectoplasmic context—
Happening again, even if
The companion who smiled in that dusk long ago, and
Smiles now again—ah, new innocence,
For now freed from Time—
Is long dead, and I
Am not always readily certain
Of the name now.

For that old *I* is not I any more, though
A ghost somewhat different from that of
The truly perished companion, for the *I* here now
Is not dead, only what
I have now turned into. This
Is the joke you must live with. Have you ever
Seen serpentine Time at the instant it swallowed its tail?

But whatever I am and Truth is, I
Have stood on a high place, yearning
To know what logic of years, and of
Whatever stride, clamber, climb,

Had brought me here to be what I am; downward,
Have seen how wind tossed wildly,
In flicker like gale-spray,
Gray undersides of innumerable leaves
Of the forest below. And whatever
Vision or anguish
Swelled in the heart to be uttered was
By wind crammed in the throat back, and all
I recall is the shadowy thought that
Man's mind, his heart, live only by piecemeal, like mice
On cheese crumbs—the cheese itself, of course,
Being locked in the tin
In God's pantry.

Well, you might, of course, go to bed, and stare
Up at the coagulate darkness and know
How beyond the frail rooftop darkness piles skyward—
Thinking now that at least you are *you*,
Saying *now*, saying *now*, for
Now *now* is all, and you *you*.

At least, for a minute.

This may be taken as an argument for prayer.

Diver

Arrowed, the body flies in light.
The heels flash as water closes.
The board yet quivers where feet struck.
Concentric to the water's wound,
In live geometry the bright-
Born circles widen targetwise
In mathematic accuracy.

Now in the water's inner gleam,
Where no sound comes, and yap and nag
Of the world's old currish annoy is stilled,
The body glides. In timeless peace
The mover that shows no movement moves
Behind the prow of a diver's hands,
And in our watching hearts we know
An unsuspected depth and calm
Of identity we had never dreamed.

But look! The face is up, dark hair
Snaps sidewise to show the boyish grin.
And we smile, too, in welcome back
To all the joy and anguish of
The earth we walk on, lie down in.

Rather Like a Dream

If Wordsworth, a boy, reached out
To touch stone or tree to confirm
His own reality, that wasn't

So crazy. Or even illogical. For
We have all done the same, or at least
Felt the impulse. Right now I feel it, for

I walk in the mountain woods,
Alone, hour sunset, season
When the first maple leaf falls red, the first

Beech leaf gold. Each leaf of each species
Gathers, brooding, beneath it, its film
Of darkness, and waits, and the promise

Of another summer is already a dream. Thus years,
As I stand at this moment, are gathered
In their brooding darkness beneath.

Another summer is now truly a dream
To join those moments, and hours, of joy
That dissolve into glitter, like tears, then gather

Each under a brooding leaf, or join
The darkness of conifers, not yet snow-draped.
I stand on stone and am thinking

Of what is no more. Oh, happiness!—often
Unrecognized. But shade hardens, and years

Are darkening under each leaf—old love, old folly,

Old evil and anguish, and the drawstring
Of darkness draws tighter, and the monk-hood
Of darkness grows like a sky over all,

As I stand in the spruce-deep where stars never come.
I stand, hands at sides, and wonder,
Wonder if I should put out a hand to touch

Tree or stone—just to know.

Departure

This is the season when cards are exchanged, or
Addresses scribbled on paper, with ragged edges. Smiles
Are frozen with a mortuary precision to seal friendships. Time is up.

The sun goes earlier low. The last sail, far out,
Looks lonely. And if, toward sunset, at low tide, you walk
Near the shoals, you will find the sea-grass

Combed scrupulously in one direction only
As if some fundamental decision,
Involving us all, had at last been reached, but

Not yet released for announcement. Tomorrow,
We shall sense the direction of history, and now, far away,
In the casino, the first cards are being cut. The dealer

Coughs, the mistral levels in, and you
Again begin to believe what you read in the papers. The market
Wiggles like a cardiogram, or an earthworm on a hot concrete walk, and

In the shadowy corridors luggage, generally expensive, is stacked. Polished
Cowhide glints with a sense of its own destiny, it knows
It is going somewhere soon. That is a truth we must all face.

Heat Wave Breaks

In this motionless sun, no leaf now moves, the stream,
In unwavering reach, mirrors sky's cloudlessness.
On a beech bough, wrapped in the forest's deepest green dream,
The warbler sits ruffled, beak open but music-less.
For some coolness the feathers are ruffled to give air ingress.

In the gasp of silence that follows your new heartbeat
Do you catch the echo of one only just now spent?
Or does Time itself, in that timeless and crystalline heat,
Hang transparent, a concept bleached of all content?
At this moment can you recall what your own life has meant?

Though no leaf moves, and the past dies in the heart,
Though no bird sings, and the sun seems nailed to the sky,
We have hope in the hour when, west, on the cliff's top rampart
The day will redden to flame, like the phoenix, to die,
And darkness come, star by star, to assume the sky.

Will you wake when clouds roll and the roil and lightning make
Again wet leaves twirl on their stems in the green-flaming glare,
And blasphemy of thunder makes the mountain quake?
For what should we pray to our God in the rumble and flare?
That the world stab anew to our hearts in the lightning-stricken air?

Heart of Autumn

Wind finds the northwest gap, fall comes.
Today, under gray cloud-scud and over gray
Wind-flicker of forest, in perfect formation, wild geese
Head for a land of warm water, the *boom*, the lead pellet.

Some crumple in air, fall. Some stagger, recover control,
Then take the last glide for a far glint of water. None
Knows what has happened. Now, today, watching
How tirelessly *V* upon *V* arrows the season's logic,

Do I know my own story? At least, they know
When the hour comes for the great wing-beat. Sky-strider,
Star-strider—they rise, and the imperial utterance,
Which cries out for distance, quivers in the wheeling sky.

That much they know, and in their nature know
The path of pathlessness, with all the joy
Of destiny fulfilling its own name.
I have known time and distance, but not why I am here.

Path of logic, path of folly, all
The same—and I stand, my face lifted now skyward,
Hearing the high beat, my arms outstretched in the tingling
Process of transformation, and soon tough legs,
    *

With folded feet, trail in the sounding vacuum of passage,
And my heart is impacted with a fierce impulse
To unwordable utterance—
Toward sunset, at a great height.

About the Author

ROBERT PENN WARREN was born in Guthrie, Kentucky, in 1905. After graduating summa cum laude from Vanderbilt University (1925), he received a master's degree from the University of California (1927) and did graduate work at Yale University (1927–28) and at Oxford as a Rhodes Scholar (B.Litt., 1930).

Mr. Warren has published many books, including ten novels, twelve volumes of poetry, a volume of short stories, a play, a collection of critical essays, a biography, two historical essays, and two studies of race relations in America. This body of work has been published in a period of forty-nine years—a period during which Mr. Warren has also had an active career as a professor of English.

All the King's Men (1946) was awarded the Pulitzer Prize for Fiction. The Shelley Memorial Award recognized Mr. Warren's early poetry. *Promises* (1957) won the Pulitzer Prize for Poetry, the Edna St. Vincent Millay Prize of the Poetry Society of America, and the National Book Award. In 1944–45 Mr. Warren was the second occupant of the Chair of Poetry at the Library of Congress. In 1952 he was elected to the American Philosophical Society; in 1959 to the American Academy of Arts and Letters; and in 1975 to the American Academy of Arts and Sciences. In 1967 he received the Bollingen Prize in Poetry for *Selected Poems: New and Old, 1923–1966,* and in 1970 the National Medal for Literature and the Van Wyck Brooks Award for the book-length poem *Audubon: A Vision.* In 1974 he was chosen by the National Endowment for the Humanities to deliver the third Annual Jefferson Lecture in the Humanities. In 1975 he received the Emerson-Thoreau Award of the American Academy of Arts and Sciences. In 1976 he received the Copernicus Award from the Academy of American Poets, in recognition of his career but with special notice of *Or Else—Poem/Poems 1968–1974.* In 1977 he received the Harriet Monroe Prize for Poetry. He is a Chancellor of the Academy of American Poets.

Mr. Warren lives in Connecticut with his wife, Eleanor Clark (author of *Rome and a Villa, The Oysters of Locmariaquer, Baldur's Gate,* and *Eyes, Etc.: A Memoir*), and their two children, Rosanna and Gabriel.